NEW ORLEANS

Contents

Irving Weisdorf & Co. Ltd.

INTRODUCTION

New Orleans has many nicknames; among them, The Big Easy and Crescent City. Whatever you call it, this city is one of the most exciting destinations in the American South. Home to some half a million people, (over one million if you count the **Greater New Orleans Metropolitan Area**) it has a distinct personality and throbs with life and color — the legacy of a rich and storied past.

During the course of its history many nationalities have left their mark. For hundreds of years, **native Americans** made New Orleans their homeland. They traveled by canoe in the swamplands around **Lake Pontchartrain** and the **Mississippi River**. The mighty river was the gateway to the **Gulf of Mexico** and in a later era, a trade route to the **Caribbean** and the rest of the world.

By the 17th century, the **French**, intent on expanding their North American empire, set their sights on this sleepy backwater. Imagining that untold riches lay in the interior — perhaps even the silver and gold that had financed the **Spanish** expeditions in **South America** — they envisaged a great and glorious city. History has since proved them right, but in 1718 only a small settlement had been established in the mosquito-infested swamps.

The driving force behind the fledgling community was a Seigneur from **New France**, **Jean Baptiste de Bienville**,

who diplomatically named the settlement in honor of the **Duke of Orleans**, then ruling France until the young king **Louis XV** came of age. The French didn't hold New Orleans for long — the Spanish took it over in 1762. **Napoleon** regained power in 1800, but only three years later, France sold the city to the **United States** in the **Louisiana Purchase**.

New Orleans developed rapidly and many nationalities, from every level of society, flocked to the shores of the Mississippi — **African slaves**, **French farmers**, **Spanish aristocrats**, **English traders**, **Indian merchants**, **Creoles** (descendants of Spanish and French settlers), **Acadians** expelled from **Canada** (in Louisiana they became known as "**Cajuns**") and a sprinkling of shady characters who didn't always operate on the right side of the law.

Its colorful population has made New Orleans one of the most cosmopolitan cities on the continent, brewing a cultural mix that seeps into every aspect of life — the culture, food, history and, of course, the music. The "joie de vivre" of its citizens is manifest in a myriad of ways including **Mardi Gras**, hot cajun cuisine, exuberant architecture and a language spiced with French, but most of all, in the laissez-faire lifestyle.

In this relaxed southern setting visitors can forget their worldly cares and just "Let the good times roll," as they say around these parts.

HISTORY / ARCHITECTURE

New Orleans is a city of neighborhoods, each with a distinct personality. They are not, as in most North American cities, laid out in neat rectangles on the grid system. Rather they have grown up around the meanderings of the Mississippi, hence the term "**Crescent City**."

The most famous and historic neighborhood is the **Vieux Carré** (Old Square) or the **French Quarter**. Tourists are drawn to the stylish architecture, specialty stores, jazz clubs and street life which make this twelve by six block area one of the liveliest in town. The city had its beginnings here and although some of the oldest buildings have been destroyed by hurricanes, floods and fires, the historic ambience prevails.

In colonial times **Jackson Square**, named for **Andrew Jackson** who drove off the British in 1815 during the **Battle of New Orleans**, was the hub of the Vieux Carré. The square was renamed after Jackson's brave stand against the English invaders but it existed long before then. The French called it **Place d'Armes**, the Spanish, **Plaza de Armas**. Originally it was used as a training ground for the militia. Today the square is peaceful and the pretty, landscaped park is surrounded by a pedestrian mall that is teeming with **street artists** and **musicians**.

Jackson Square is a good place to start exploring the French Quarter. Dominated by the distinctive St. Louis Cathedral, Jackson Square is easy to find.

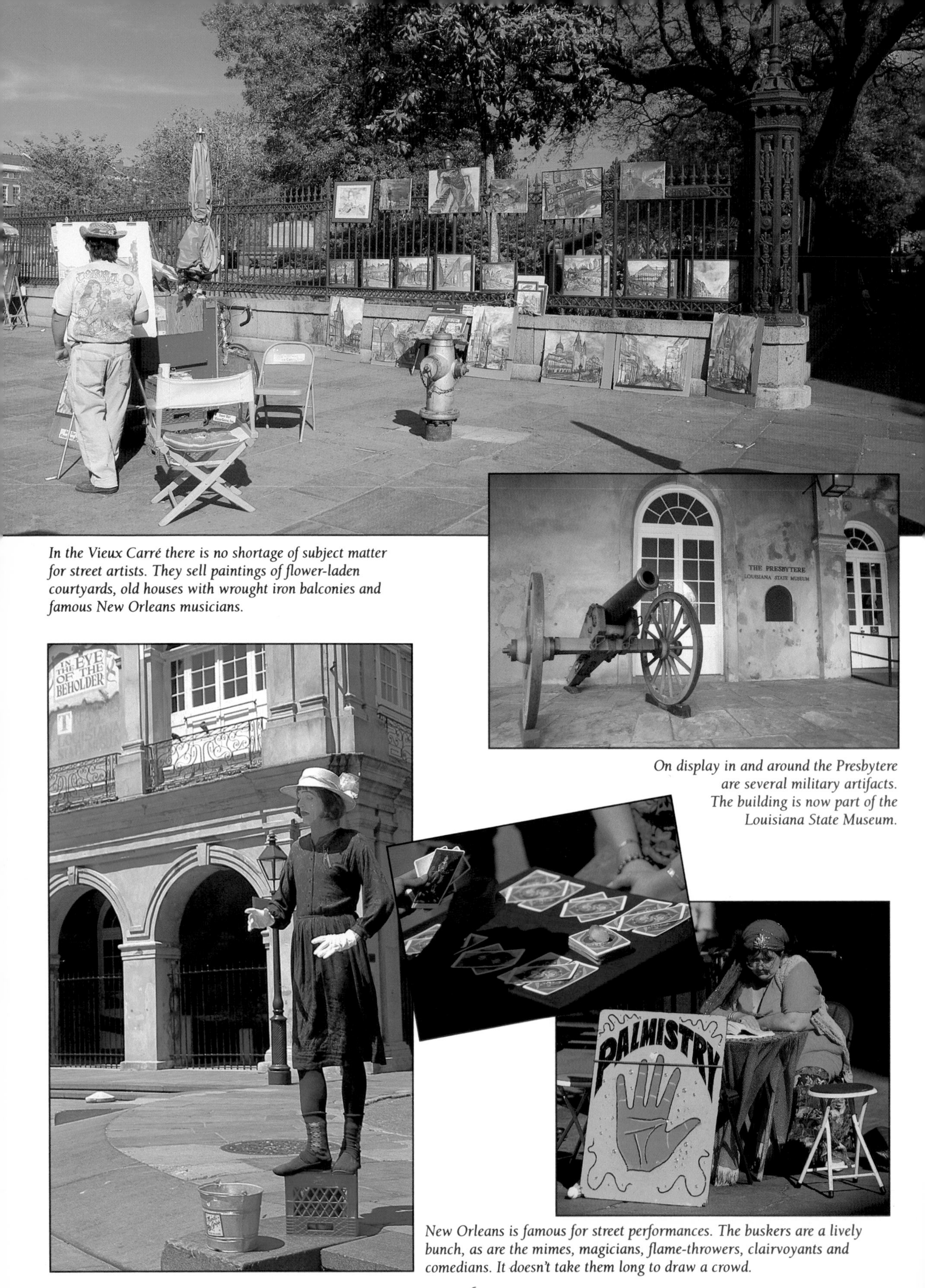

In the Vieux Carré there is no shortage of subject matter for street artists. They sell paintings of flower-laden courtyards, old houses with wrought iron balconies and famous New Orleans musicians.

On display in and around the Presbytere are several military artifacts. The building is now part of the Louisiana State Museum.

New Orleans is famous for street performances. The buskers are a lively bunch, as are the mimes, magicians, flame-throwers, clairvoyants and comedians. It doesn't take them long to draw a crowd.

Andrew Jackson is revered as a hero in New Orleans because his ragtag army defeated the more professional British forces. To outsiders he's better known as the seventh president of the United States. The 14-foot bronze statue of the statesman is the most photographed monument in the city.

The Cabildo, with its handsome arches, is typical of the many architectural styles found in the French Quarter. In 1803, French and American officials met in a chamber on the second floor to sign the Louisiana Purchase.

The **Cabildo** and the **Presbytere**, two distinctive buildings with elegant archways, colonnades and mansard roofs, dominate Jackson Square. The Cabildo ("council") was the meeting place of the Spanish rulers. The Presbytere, as its name suggests, was built to house the clergy. Later it became a courthouse.

A statue of Andrew Jackson mounted on a rearing horse stands in front of the triple-spired **St. Louis Cathedral**, the oldest in the United States. It was named after the saintly **Louis IX** who commanded two holy crusades. This building dates back to 1794, when it replaced two earlier churches which were destroyed by a hurricane and a fire.

In 1964, the cathedral was elevated to the status of **basilica**, one of only 15 churches so honored in the country. When **Pope John Paul II** held a mass here in 1987, the pedestrian mall in front of the cathedral was renamed **Place Jean Paul Deux** in his honor. The cathedral is open to the public and worshippers are always welcome.

Jean Lafitte and his brother Pierre ran contraband rackets in New Orleans. At one point the American government pardoned Pierre because he refused to join the British Navy despite a sizeable bribe. Jean, however, did not show such loyalty. He moved from New Orleans and promptly became a pirate once again in what is now Galveston, Texas.

There's a colorful legend connected with **Lafitte's Blacksmith Shop**. Local lore claims that this pretty old cottage was once the headquarters of pirate **Jean Lafitte**. The blacksmith's shop was said to be a front for his illegal operations, though documents have never been found to prove it. It really doesn't matter, the place has been a bar for many years. Playwright **Tennessee Williams** was once a regular customer.

Whether or not you believe the legends, from an architectural and historical point of view, Lafitte's Blacksmith Shop is very interesting. Erected in 1772, it is one of the few remaining examples of the construction techniques used by early settlers — brick reinforced by timber.

Another fine example of **French Creole** architecture is the **1752 Old Ursuline Convent**, a three-story stone building with a steep roof and dormer windows. Surrounded by a formal garden with lawns and hedges trimmed in geometric designs, it was the only major institution to survive the ravaging fires that swept through New Orleans in the 1700s.

Wealthy New Orleans aristocrats — the Creoles — sent their children to be educated at the Old Ursuline Convent. They were taught by the Sisters of St. Ursula who came to New Orleans in 1727.

EXIT
EXIT
EXIT

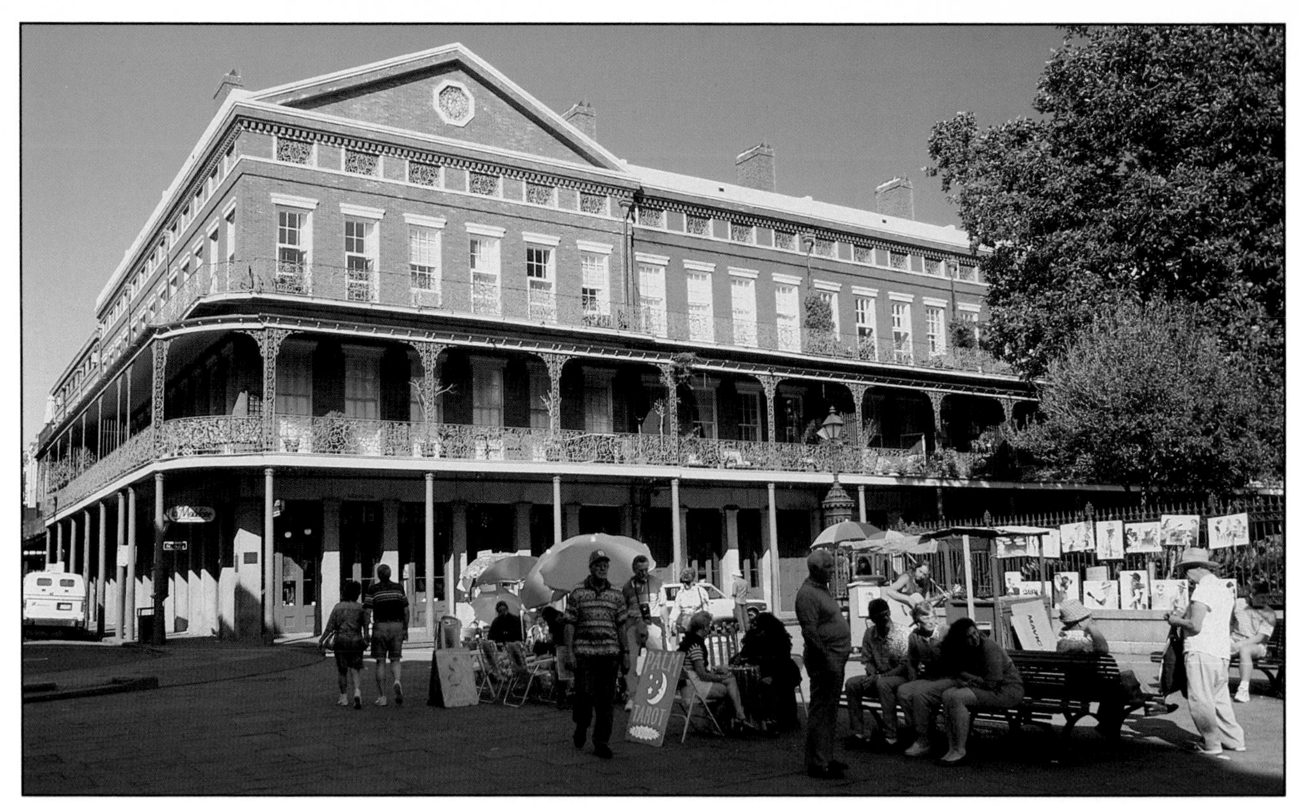

Baroness Micaela Pontalba, after whom the Pontalba Apartments are named, caused a fearful scandal in the 1840s by having a fight with her father-in-law, then marching out on her husband. Her behavior created shock waves around Europe, as well as in Louisiana.

Novelist Frances Parkinson Keyes, who once lived in the Beauregard-Keyes house, is best known for "Dinner at Antoine's" penned at her studio. Her beautiful home was evidently a source of great inspiration. She completed 40 books here, all of them written in longhand.

The **Gallier House** belongs to a more recent era. Built in 1857 by architect **James Gallier Jr.**, it is one of the best examples of an 18th-century townhouse in the city. The house has been restored to its original condition and is now a museum operated by **Tulane University**.

Not far from the Gallier House, on Royal Street, is the **Labranche House**, a striking illustration of New Orleans' early 19th-century architecture. The house, one of the most photographed in the city, is ringed with a curved balcony made of the wrought iron "lace," typical of New Orleans in the 1830s.

Beauregard-Keyes House is another handsome home from the 19th century. Its name is from two famous owners — **General P.G.T. Beauregard**, who moved here after the **American Civil War**, and novelist **Frances Parkinson Keyes**, who restored the house in the 1940s. The home has an elegant, pillared facade and a walled garden which blooms all year round.

The most striking features of Labranche House are the multi-level patterned balconies. A close look reveals oak leaves and acorns woven into the ironwork.

The 19th-century Gallier House which has servants' quarters, is a museum filled with period furnishings such as antique clocks, crystal chandeliers, silverware, porcelain dishes and marble fireplaces. Chairs are upholstered in velvet and brocade.

The red brick **Pontalba Apartments** were built as private homes but also housed stores and offices — an innovative concept in the mid-1800s. The apartments, which are among the oldest in the United States, were financed by the strong-willed **Baroness Micaela Almonester Rojas**, daughter of a wealthy Spaniard. She became a member of the gentry after marrying her cousin, **Baron Celestin de Pontalba**.

The baroness, who inherited the land on which the apartments are built, quickly seized an economic opportunity. At the time she built her mixed residential and commercial complex, people were pouring into the city to start new enterprises. Baroness Pontalba also donated sizeable sums of money to landscape **Jackson Square** and erect the statue of Jackson within it. The Pontalba buildings still house stores on the ground floor and premium apartments above.

The iron balconies which adorn the Pontalba Apartments were molded rather than individually worked, a technique introduced by the indefatiguable baroness. She also made sure her name would be remembered. The letters "A" and "P" for **Almonester** and **Pontalba**, are worked into the iron design.

The graceful curves, pillars and delicate iron lacework of the balconies in the **French Quarter** are among the most photographed architectural features in the old city. The earliest balconies were forged from wrought iron. The most recent ones are cast, but only architectural purists would quibble about such details.

The balconies are beautiful and they conjur up the character of the Vieux Carré. They provide the perfect vantage point from which to watch the busy street life down below. Festooned with hanging flowers, they also provide welcome shade on hot, humid days, that are by no means rare in New Orleans.

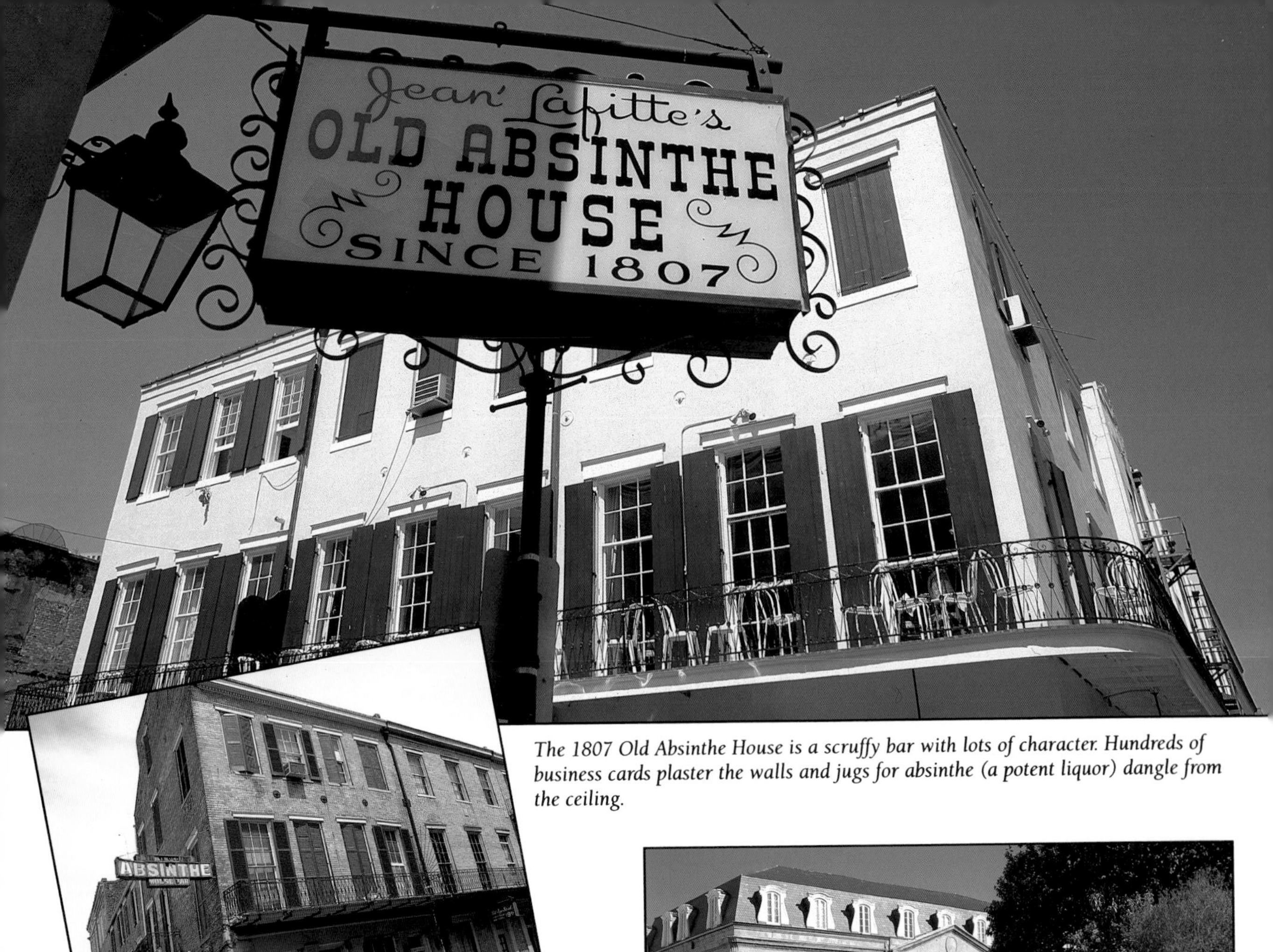

The 1807 Old Absinthe House is a scruffy bar with lots of character. Hundreds of business cards plaster the walls and jugs for absinthe (a potent liquor) dangle from the ceiling.

The Presbytere stands to the right of St. Louis Cathedral and is part of the Louisiana State Museum. Exhibits highlight local culture and maritime history.

The **Old Absinthe House**, a popular tavern, is another site connected with pirate Jean Lafitte. Like Lafitte's Blacksmith Shop, however, the connection is probably more fiction than fact. What *is* known is that the building dates back to 1807. The **Hermann-Grima House** at 820 St. Louis Street is more reliably documented. This building is an example of early American, rather than French, architecture and is one of the best preserved homes in New Orleans.

During the **American Civil War** the **Confederacy** issued its currency at the **Old U.S. Mint**, part of the **Louisiana State Museum** complex, but few coins have survived. Still, the museum has many other interesting exhibits. Music lovers will particularly enjoy the exhibits relating to Mardi Gras and the origins of **New Orleans Jazz**.

In addition to the U.S. Mint, at 400 Esplanade Avenue, the Louisiana State Museum encompasses the **1850 House**, the **Presbytere** and the **Cabildo**. The 1850 House, at 523 St. Ann Street, is a recreated antebellum town house.

Napoleon House, as its name suggests, was intended as a home for **Napoleon Bonaparte**. The house belonged to New Orleans mayor **Nicholas Girod** who sympathised with the exiled French dictator and wanted to provide him with a safe haven. Girod, along with some other fans of the ousted ruler, renovated the house in readiness for Napoleon's arrival, but he never made it. He died in **St. Helena**, in 1821.

Madame John's Legacy is associated with another colorful character, though this one is drawn from fiction. The lady in question was a freed slave who was the heroine of a short story by George Washington Cable. It tells the tale of how Madame John became the mistress of a wealthy Frenchman — not an unusual scenario in these parts — who on his death bed, bequeathed her his home and estate.

Local writers and artists hang out at Napoleon House, a bar and cafe where it's easy to imagine the romance of a bygone era.

Within the Old U.S. Mint are the Mardi Gras Museum and the New Orleans Jazz Collection. The Mardi Gras exhibits include the masks, floats and extravagant costumes used during the annual festivities.

Madame John's Legacy is not open to the public, but even from the outside visitors can imagine an earlier era.

Judge Felix Grima purchased this home from Samuel Hermann and his descendants lived here through five generations. The family lived a very comfortable life, as the elegant furnishings indicate.

The kitchen in the Hermann-Grima House is restored to the style of the 1830s. Guides show visitors how food was prepared with simple utensils, then cooked over an open fire.

Samuel Hermann, a rich merchant, was the original owner of the Hermann-Grima House. With its handsome brick exterior and shuttered windows, it is considered to be the finest example of American architecture in the French Quarter and is a National Historic Landmark.

STEAK PIT
GURU
ALAMO FLAGS
611 BOURBON ST.
BUON GIORNO CAFE

LIFE

THE NAME "BOURBON" POPS UP ALL OVER THE FRENCH Quarter and not just because of the famous street which dissects the Vieux Carré from east to west. **Bourbon Street** is one of the liveliest thoroughfares in the nation and is lined with nightclubs, bars, jazz joints and terrific restaurants serving **Creole** and **Cajun** foods.

Given Bourbon Street's reputation as a night spot you might think it was named after the strong rye-whiskey made in Kentucky, but it actually refers to the French royal family who ruled over Louisiana for almost a century. The best known member of the **Bourbon dynasty** was the "**Sun King" Louis XIV**, who held the throne when French explorers from Canada made their first forays into New Orleans.

In New Orleans people can party all night. The city is one of only two in the United States (the other is Las Vegas), which does not have a closing law.

Bourbon Street, in more recent times, was the place that gave birth to **Dixieland Jazz**. At the turn of the century, musicians who played this infectious, rolling music would gather in Bourbon Street and other New Orleans venues to practise their craft. The music started in a simple way. Evolving from **gospel harmonies**, it soon became the most distinctive local sound.

Traditional jazz is still popular on Bourbon Street and it booms from the clubs and pubs that line the sidewalks. Some of the eateries and taverns feature **live musicians**. Others just play recorded music, but jazz and blues blares from almost every doorway, putting passersby into a party mood.

Bourbon Street comes alive at night when revelers lurch from one bar to another in search of entertainment.

A walk down Bourbon Street is not for the faint-hearted. Voodoo Shops are among the weird and wonderful establishments.

The restaurants along Bourbon Street specialize in local fare, like fresh seafood, gumbo (a soup made from okra), crawfish and tongue-tingling Cajun stews.

Royal Street is aptly named. It is one of the classiest stretches of real estate in the Vieux Carré. Here, as in other parts of the French Quarter, are renovated buildings but these are more elegant than some of the tawdry establishments on nearby Bourbon Street.

The Jackson Brewery, a striking white building near the waterfront, provides spectacular views of the French Quarter and the Mississippi River.

The apartments along Decatur Street, like those in most parts of the Vieux Carré, are very much in demand.

Decatur Street runs parallel with Bourbon Street, three blocks to the south. In the middle of the street is Jackson Square and to the south is the **French Market**. At its eastern end are the **Ursuline Convent** and the **U.S. Mint**, three major tourist attractions which can easily be explored on foot.

From Decatur Street it's an easy stroll to Royal Street. It is indeed a "royal" experience to wander here. The elegant old buildings have been turned into art galleries and antique shops. Even if you're not buying it's fun to window shop. Half way along Royal Street is **Pirate's Alley**, a lane flanking the St. Louis Cathedral. It's named after buccaneer Jean Lafitte, who is said to have planned the **1815 Battle of New Orleans** here.

In the **Jackson Brewery**, just east of the French Market, are a couple of popular venues found in many places around the globe — **Planet Hollywood** and the **Hard Rock Cafe**. They are just two of the over 70 shops and restaurants in this entertainment and retail complex. **JAX**, a local beer, was manufactured in the brewery until the 1970s.

STEVE
FRAMING
523-4146

738

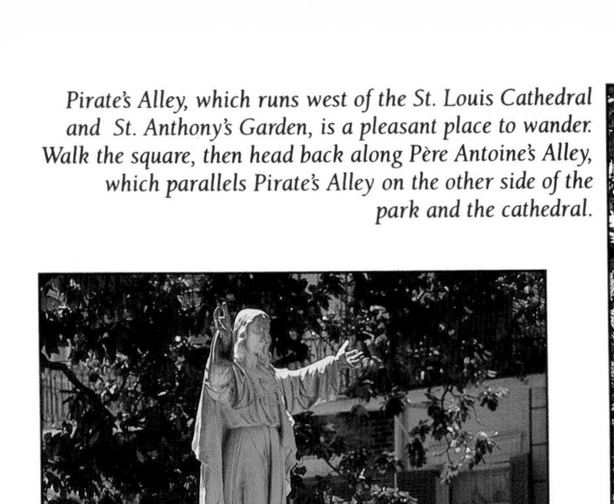

Pirate's Alley, which runs west of the St. Louis Cathedral and St. Anthony's Garden, is a pleasant place to wander. Walk the square, then head back along Père Antoine's Alley, which parallels Pirate's Alley on the other side of the park and the cathedral.

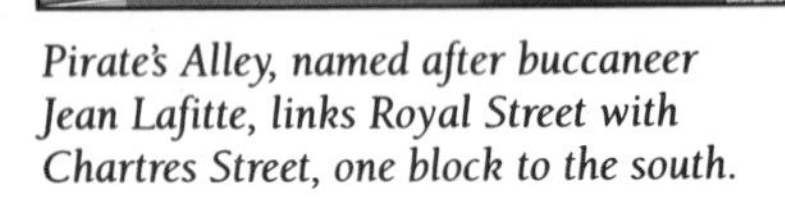

Pirate's Alley, named after buccaneer Jean Lafitte, links Royal Street with Chartres Street, one block to the south.

Street artists display their work along Pirate's Alley. At night this romantic walkway is a favorite place for lovers seeking a quiet place to stroll and chat.

The **French Market** is an interesting spot to while away a couple of hours. You can find all manner of merchandise for sale; from alligator heads to trinkets from Taiwan.

The French Market has been here since the early days. It was a trading post for native Americans long before Europeans arrived. When the French and Spanish ruled New Orleans it was a bustling, open-air market and the commercial center of the **Vieux Carré**. There are still some

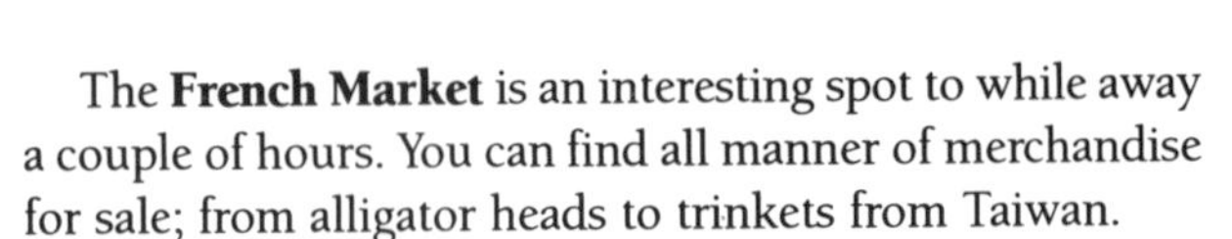

The French Market is a meeting place for locals and tourists alike and has been the heart and soul of the Vieux Carré for over two centuries.

A stroll through the French Market is an assault on the senses. Unique and colorful merchandise dazzles the eyes, while the heady odor of cheese, chocolate and fresh-brewed coffee play at the noses of visitors.

At some of the seafood stalls, vendors will package the food with ice so it can be carried on airplanes or in cars.

The French Market stretches five blocks and encompasses many kinds of commercial establishments including a farmers' market, a flea market, gift shops, upscale restaurants and outdoor cafes with live jazz.

At the French Market, shoppers can find everything from fresh fruit and vegetables to strange souvenirs like alligator heads.

open-air stalls and the market hums with life, but many of the shops and food concessions are now inside a complex of renovated buildings.

Give yourself a treat and stop by **Café du Monde**, the restaurant at the entrance of the French Market. The cafe, which has been in business since 1860, is open 24-hours per day and is known for delicious beignets — rectangular donuts drenched in sugar. The place is always crowded, even very early in the morning, when revelers returning from a night on the skids, try to clear their heads with a sugar fix and steaming mugs of cafe au lait, laced with chicory — New Orleans style.

Street entertainers are part of the summer landscape in many North American cities, but in New Orleans the tradition goes back a long way. Music has been part of the local scene since the birth of Dixieland at the turn of the century when groups of musicians performed at weddings, funerals, christenings and confirmations, most of which were held outdoors.

Much of the street entertainment is free, or at least costs only the price of a couple of coins dropped into a hat or open violin case. There are numerous clubs and restaurants where visitors can hear jazz and other kinds of music. Many of the street musicians are considerably more talented than the headliners in the clubs.

The French Market and Jackson Square are the two main venues where performers cluster. Using the street as a stage, anything goes, from **jugglers** and **flame throwers**, to **puppets** playing the piano. Musicians compete with one another to produce the most unusual sounds, playing everything from tubas to washboards. **Clowns** and **balloon men** entertain the kids, making them yell with glee every time they perform a trick.

St. Loui
FINE JEWELRY
YIELD
LET'S GET PHYSICAL
CAFÉ DU MONDE · THE ORIGINAL COFFEE STAND

New Orleanians will use any excuse to stage a festival and throughout the year there are dozens of celebrations. There's at least one festival every week, from the whimsically named **Reggae Riddums Festival** held in June, to the **Swamp Festival** in early October, which highlights Cajun food, music and crafts. Even the lowly tomato is celebrated with cooking demonstrations during the annual **Great French Market Tomato Festival** held in early June.

In mid-April the French Quarter stages its annual celebration. The **French Quarter Festival** highlights the music and food of New Orleans. Thirteen stages are set up for free entertainment throughout the Vieux Carré and revelers can wander from one site to another. Events are staged for children and there are patio tours and a fireworks show over the Mississippi River.

Fireworks soaring in a shower of stars over the Mississippi River during the French Quarter Festival, held in mid-April.

The entertainment is free during the French Quarter festival. Music is performed by brass bands, piano players, trombonists and anyone else who can lay their hands on an instrument.

Woldenberg Riverfront Park, which connects to Moon Walk, is livelier than usual during the French Quarter Festival.

Plants provide a splash of greenery in a part of town where space is at a premium. Locals may not have room for a large garden, but they can always find a spot on a patio or a wall for a flower pot or two.

Among the most charming architectural features of the French Quarter's homes are the **courtyards** and **patio gardens** which are often hidden from public view. One of the delights of strolling around the old town is suddenly coming across one of these courtyards, hidden behind a wall, or glimpsed through the archway of a private home.

The courtyards are similar to those found around some of the classier small hotels in **Paris** which were built as city residences by **French nobles** in the 17th and 18th centuries. Indeed, some of the small, **European-style** hotels in the Vieux Carré echo that architectural style.

In a part of the city where space is at a premium and where few people have large gardens, courtyards shrouded in greenery provide a welcome oasis from the heat and humidity. The New Orleans climate allows plants to grow as abundantly as in the **Caribbean**.

CULTURE

PARTY TIME IS ALL THE TIME IN NEW ORLEANS AND THE biggest party of all is **Mardi Gras**, the culmination of **Carnival** which starts on **Epiphany** (January 6). Mardi Gras (Fat Tuesday in French) is a day of wild revelry, a preparation for lent, a six-week period before **Easter**.

New Orleans' version of Mardi Gras no doubt evolved from the customs of its European rulers. The first documented celebration was in 1857 when a private club known as the **Mystick Krewe of Comus** staged a grand, costumed ball. Several other groups originating in the last century still stage formal masked balls where debutantes are presented to society and attendance is by invitation only.

The Mardi Gras celebrations have evolved way beyond their origins and now everybody can join in the fun. During the two weeks leading up to the Mardi Gras weekend dozens of dances and over 100 balls are run by non-profit groups who appoint Carnival "kings" and "queens" to preside over the proceedings. Their identity is always kept secret until the day before Mardi Gras.

Some of the newer "krewes," such as **Bacchus** and **Endymion**, organize public suppers with celebrities rather than carnival kings and queens. **Bob Hope**, **Billy Crystal**, **Neil Sedaka**, **Dolly Parton** and **Harry Connick Jr.** have all been participants.

In the 12 days leading up to Mardi Gras more than 60 **parades** with lavishly **decorated floats**, **costumed entertainers**, **brass bands**, **motorcycle teams** and **horses** wind through the city and suburbs. Everybody and everything is decked out to the nines. Buildings all over town are draped with Carnival colors of green, representing faith, purple, for justice, and gold which indicates power.

The parades help set the stage for Mardi Gras and crank up the excitement which culminates Tuesday, when the entire city goes completely wild. More than one million people take to the streets, clad in the wildest outfits imaginable. Even the police don wigs and sunglasses.

When a float comes into view crowds start yelling for "**throws**," trinkets tossed by participants in the parades. They are simple momentoes — plastic drinking cups, beads, medallions, doubloons (aluminum coins) and the like — but visitors caught up in the party spirit shout as if they were being given silver or gold. "Throw me something mister!" is the battlecry of Mardi Gras, one of the most noisy and exciting celebrations on the continent.

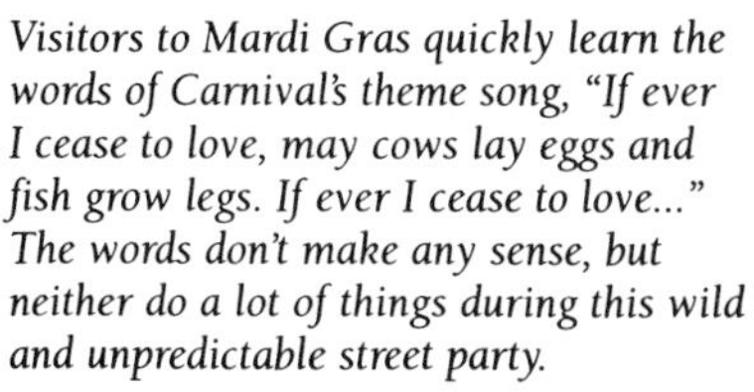

Visitors to Mardi Gras quickly learn the words of Carnival's theme song, "If ever I cease to love, may cows lay eggs and fish grow legs. If ever I cease to love..." The words don't make any sense, but neither do a lot of things during this wild and unpredictable street party.

All the krewes that participate in Mardi Gras select their own kings and queens, but the reigning monarchs are Rex and his Queen, chosen by the prestigious School of Design. The Rex parade is Carnival's main event.

350 decorated floats take part in the parades organized by the Rex, Argus and Grela krewes during Mardi Gras. Over 14,000 costumed revelers dance, yell and sing to the waiting crowds as the floats wind through the streets.

Eating out is one of the great pleasures of a visit to New Orleans. The city has over **2,500 restaurants** and the variety of foods they serve is staggering. Although you can find dishes from virtually any corner of the world, if you like regional food, you won't be disappointed.

New Orleans is known for two particular types of cuisine, Cajun and Creole. **Creole** cooking is derived from the dishes once prepared by Spanish and French aristocrats and their servants. A more refined and hotter style of cooking than its Cajun counterpart, Creole cuisine makes good use of the abundance of seafood found in and around the Mississippi River; crawfish, flounder, redfish and oysters.

Cajun cooking is rustic, rib-sticking fare. It tends to be heavy, reflecting its simple, peasant origins. Like Creole, Cajun cuisine incorporates fish and seafood, but Cajun chefs also use duck, chicken, pork and spicy sausage laced with a hearty gravy known as roux, a mixture of fat and flour.

New Orleanians have always enjoyed their regional food but **chef Paul Prudhomme** helped put Creole-Cajun cuisine on the map. In the 1980s, his blackened redfish became the rage and popped up on menus all over the place. Thanks to Prudhomme and others like him, the popularity of southern Louisiana food has spread far beyond its borders.

New Orleans has hundreds of restaurants, from small, sidewalk cafes, to elegant eateries where formal dress is required.

The most famous voodoo queens were the two Marie Laveaus, a mother and daughter team who terrified those who believed in their supernatural powers. Marie Laveau senior was said to be the illegitimate daughter of a wealthy planter. She would ruthlessly deal with competitors by putting a curse on them — apparently with some degree of success. Marie and her daughter are buried in the Laveau-Glapion tomb in the St. Louis Cemetery #1, near the Basin Street entrance. The tomb is often adorned with candles, votive offerings and flowers left by faithful believers.

Voodoo shops sell lotions and potions said to improve the health and sex life of users. Creations include Love Oil, Controlling Powder, Get-Together Drops and Box Fix Powder.

The New Orleans Historic Voodoo Museum at 724 Dumaine Street, is filled with strange artifacts associated with voodoo — the jawbone of an ass, a number of skulls and a stuffed snake. The gift shop sells voodoo dolls and gris-gris, amulets designed to ward off evil spirits.

The very word "**voodoo**" sends shivers up the spine and conjurs up all kinds of occult practises — live animal sacrifices, drinking blood and half-naked dancers cavorting with snakes, to the sound of hypnotic drumming. Devotees of voodoo, which means "god" in the language of **Dahomey**, were said to mix magic potions and wear gris-gris, amulets designed to bring the bearer good luck or harm to their enemies.

Voodoo was a religion imported by slaves from **Africa** (it originated in what is now the **Republic of Benin**) and it incorporated a multitude of gods, rituals and cults. When the Africans brought their religion to New Orleans, it came into contact with **Roman Catholicism**, incorporating some of its beliefs. What emerged was a more benign faith which continues to hold sway over a small number of devotees.

In the 18th and 19th centuries voodoo was the "**New Age**" religion of its day and it held the upper classes in its grip. They were afraid of this "primitive" African religion and its ability to attract a mass following, particularly among the poor. Voodoo had its own hierarchy who held sway over the wealthy but superstitious Creoles — the **witch doctors** and **voodoo queens** who told fortunes, put curses on enemies and sold love potions, anything that could earn them a dollar.

Preservation Hall is one of the most popular hangouts for jazz fans in New Orleans. It isn't unusual to line up for a couple of hours before being admitted. Doors open at 8 p.m. but those in the know get there at least half an hour early.

Music is the lifeblood of New Orleans and visitors can barely walk a block without hearing **jazz**, **gospel**, **zydeco** or **rhythm and blues**, all of which have roots here. Most musical establishments are on Bourbon, Toulouse and Decatur streets in the French Quarter, but you can hear music all over the city, especially during the many festivals which New Orleans hosts throughout the year. The New Orleans **Jazz & Heritage Festival**, which is held in late April/early May is a popular event.

Jazz emerged from the New Orleans music scene at the turn of the century and by the 1920s, it had really taken

Bourbon Street comes into its element after dark. Many of the bars feature live entertainment and some stay open all night.

Along Bourbon Street, the scent of jasmine mingles with the hot sounds of jazz and rhythm and blues — a heady, exotic mix that makes New Orleans such a seductive city.

This statue commemorates Louis Armstrong, a native son who became one of the greatest jazz musicians in the world. Largely self-taught, Armstrong learned how to play the bugle and clarinet when he was quite young, mastering them both then became a virtuoso trumpeter and vocalist.

root. Its influence grew beyond the city, thanks to local artistes who became known internationally, such as **Jelly Roll Morton**, **Sidney Bechet** and **Louis Armstrong**.

Armstrong was born into poverty on August 4, 1901 and raised in a New Orleans orphanage, but he went on to become one of the greatest performers in the world. "**Satchmo**" as the trumpet player was sometimes called, raised jazz improvisation and scat singing to a fine art, setting the standard for other musicians. New Orleans continues to produce world-class jazz performers like **Harry Connick Jr.**, and the enormously talented **Marsalis family**.

Jazz isn't the only music for which New Orleans is famous. The city has hundreds of **gospel groups** and visitors can hear rhythm and blues and zydeco bands in many clubs and pubs. Rhythm and Blues, which was pioneered by **Fats Domino** in the 50s, is played in places like **Tipitina's**, **Mid-City Lanes & Sports** and the **House of Blues**. Visitors can enjoy toe-tapping zydeco sounds at the **Maple Leaf Bar** or at **Mulate's**, which bills itself as the "World's Most Famous Cajun Restaurant."

The Pharmacy Museum has a lovely walled courtyard. Medicinal plants and herbs are grown here, as when the museum was the home of Louis J. Dufilho, America's first licensed chemist.

Visitors can take guided tours of the Merieult House which was once a private home. The museum contains over 300,000 documents and photographs which record the history of the South.

The **New Orleans Museum of Art** (NOMA) is itself a work of art. Its handsome, neo-classisical facade, flanked by pillars, is reminiscent of the Parthenon. Designed by architect **Samuel Marx**, NOMA is considered to be one of the leading art galleries in the country. The museum, which specializes in **pre-Columbian**, **African** and **local art**, houses over 35,000 oils, watercolors, artifacts and sculptures.

The **Pharmacy Museum** at 514 Chartres Street, used to be the home of **Louis J. Dufilho**, America's first licensed chemist. He lived here in the 1820s and grew herbs and plants in his courtyard which he used as the base for medicines. His pharmacy, filled with antique jars, gives visitors a peek at some of the rather horrendous health remedies that were popular at the time. On display are leech jars, hair tonic (also drunk as an aphrodisiac), primitive surgery tools and a drill, used to bore holes in patients' skulls to alleviate headaches.

Practices and culture of the past also come alive at the **Historic New Orleans Collection**, part of which is a research center. Private archives, gathered by the late **Kemper** and **Leila Williams**, record the culture and history of the south with thousands of books, documents and photographs. The collection is inside the **1792 Merieult House** and the neighboring cottage at 553 Royal Street, which was the Williams' home.

Among the items on display at the New Orleans Museum of Art is a bronze sculpture by Auguste Rodin.

The Louisiana Children's Museum features challenging, interactive exhibits that entertain children for hours.

Visitors wishing to learn about the early days in Louisiana should explore the four historic buildings that comprise the Louisiana State Museum.

Former commercial buildings in the Warehouse District have been spruced up with wall murals. Artists have moved into the area and opened art galleries and shops.

Youngsters aren't likely to find the archives too interesting but they will enjoy the **Louisiana Children's Museum**, with its miniature hospital, grocery store and "hands-on" exhibits. Here children can pull levers, push knobs and play with computers. They can role play too, by pretending to be a television anchor or the captain of a tug boat.

The **Louisiana State Museum** comprises several historical buildings, all located in the French Quarter within walking distance of one another. Louisiana's cultural heritage is documented at the **Presbytere**, and in the nearby **Cabildo** visitors can learn about the early days of settlement. The **Old U.S. Mint** houses the **New Orleans Jazz Collection** and the **Mardi Gras Museum**, and the **1850 House** is a restored, antebellum home.

The culture of the past wasn't all gentility and refinement. A century-and-a-half ago the **Warehouse District** rang with the shouts of sweating workers loading cotton and other merchandise onto barges. This area, which lies between St. Charles Avenue and the Mississippi River, has many restored private homes and commercial establishments and has become the focus of a thriving arts community. After the **1984 World's Fair**, entrepreneurs started renovating the old warehouses and offices, turning them into **coffee houses**, **art galleries** and **museums**.

THE RIVERFRONT

THE **FLAMINGO CASINO** HAS 75 GAMING TABLES, 1,300 slot machines, video poker and other assorted games of chance. The casino operates on board what looks like a traditional Mississippi **sternwheeler**. Before Louisiana changed the laws to permit gaming on land, casino-operators got around the rules by running their businesses on boats — technically "floating" and able to move, rather than having a fixed address.

The riverfront includes many other tourist attractions. A major drawing card is the **Aquarium of the Americas**, a striking, cylindrical-shaped building with glass walls, at the foot of Canal Street. Before going inside take time to wander around the 16-acre **Woldenberg Park** which surrounds the Aquarium complex. From here there is a great

The Flamingo Casino is a floating gaming hall with four decks of tables and games. One deck is designated for non-smokers.

view of the Mississippi River. The waterway has changed since **Mark Twain** wrote his best-selling book, "Life on the Mississippi." But his opening words, written a century ago, still ring true, "The Mississippi is not a commonplace river, but on the contrary is in all ways remarkable..."

The creatures who live in the aquarium are remarkable too. Over 7,000 sea creatures swim around in tanks, the biggest of which holds 500,000 gallons of water. There are four themed display areas, the **Amazon River Basin**, the **Caribbean Reef**, the **Gulf Coast** and the **Mississippi River**. The design of some tanks allows visitors to eye some of the water world's most fearsome creatures, like the huge sharks who drift by like silent missiles seeking their target.

In the Caribbean Reef display at the Aquarium of the Americas, visitors watch colorful tropical sea creatures.

The Colonnade Market, the Levee Market and Bon Fête are inside Riverwalk, a festive, half-mile marketplace.

Creole Queen Paddlewheeler.

The river boats moored along the water's edge are tourist attractions, rather than the real thing, but their traditional designs conjur up the sternwheelers of yesteryear. **The Cajun Queen**, which leaves from the Aquarium of the America's dock, takes sightseers past the French Quarter, then sails by plantation homes and the site of the **Battle of New Orleans**. Evening sightseeing trips with dinner and live jazz can be enjoyed on board the **Creole Queen Paddlewheeler** and the **Natchez**, an authentic sternwheeler.

Moon Walk is a pleasant promenade along the levée which leads to **Woldenberg Riverfront Park**. The wooden walkway is dotted with benches where strollers rest and watch tugboats, barges, ferries, sailboats, freighters and cruise ships that ply the busy river.

Near the **World Trade Center**, **Riverwalk** is a three-story shopping complex with more than 200 stores and restaurants. Push cart vendors sell their wares outside the more fancy retail outlets like Eddie Bauer, Banana Republic and The Body Shop. Strolling musicians add a touch of pizzaz to shopping here, as does the view of the Mississippi which shoppers can enjoy through the glass walls.

The **Port of New Orleans** is unusual in that it's a fair distance from the sea, but it's one of the busiest and most important shipping centers in the United States. Port authorities control 22 miles of wharves and terminals along the Mississippi River which process more than 30 million tons of cargo every year.

Bright red antique streetcars travel a two-mile route along the Mississippi River. They make eight stops between Esplanade Avenue in the French Quarter, and the New Orleans Convention Center on Julia Street.

The Old Man River statue by Robert Schoen stands 18 feet tall near Jackson Square, on the bank of the Mississippi. The 12-ton river god is carved from white marble imported from Carrara, Italy.

Seventy shipping lines transit the Port of New Orleans. Commodities processed through the harbor include iron, steel, coffee, tea, rubber and sugar.

Moon Walk is named after Moon Candrieu, who was the mayor of New Orleans when the walk was built in the 1970s.

The World Trade Center, across from the Spanish Plaza, is the headquarters for dozens of consulates and international trade offices. Colorful flags from a multitude of nations hang in the windows.

The Canal Street Ferry provides a spectacular view of the New Orleans skyline as it crosses the powerful Mississippi River to Algiers.

The **Canal Street ferry**, which swishes back and forth to **Algiers**, a 20-minute crossing, gives visitors yet another great overview of the waterfront. It's also one of the cheapest boat rides going. There's a nominal fee for vehicles and pedestrians ride free.

When your feet get tired, jump aboard one of the trolleys. The **vintage streetcars** make several stops in the **French Quarter**, the **Central Business District** and **Warehouse District**.

BUSINESS

THE CENTRAL BUSINESS DISTRICT, OR CBD AS LOCALS refer to it, is the commercial heart of New Orleans. The city is not just a major tourist attraction but also an important manufacturing and service center. It has the second busiest port in the United States and is a transhipment point for all kinds of raw goods and manufactured materials.

Imports which are processed through the city include bananas, cocoa, coffee and bauxite, much of which comes from **Latin America**. Goods moving out of New Orleans include cotton, grain and food products. They are shipped down the Mississippi River, into the **Gulf of Mexico** and from there, around the world.

The city's industrial base is very diversified and hundreds of manufacturers, engage in everything from petroleum refining to the production of wood products. In the Central Business District the **banks**, **insurance offices**, **hotels** and **highrise business centers** are the focus of most of the commerce.

The Central Business District begins at the foot of **Canal Street** and sprawls from the Mississippi River to **Loyola Avenue**. Around Loyola Avenue is the **Duncan Plaza Civic Center**, the **City Hall** and the **Louisiana Superdome**, home of the **New Orleans Saints** football team. Canal Street marks the division between the Central Business District and the French Quarter. Locals refer to the CBD as "uptown" or "upriver," and the French Quarter as "downtown" or "downriver."

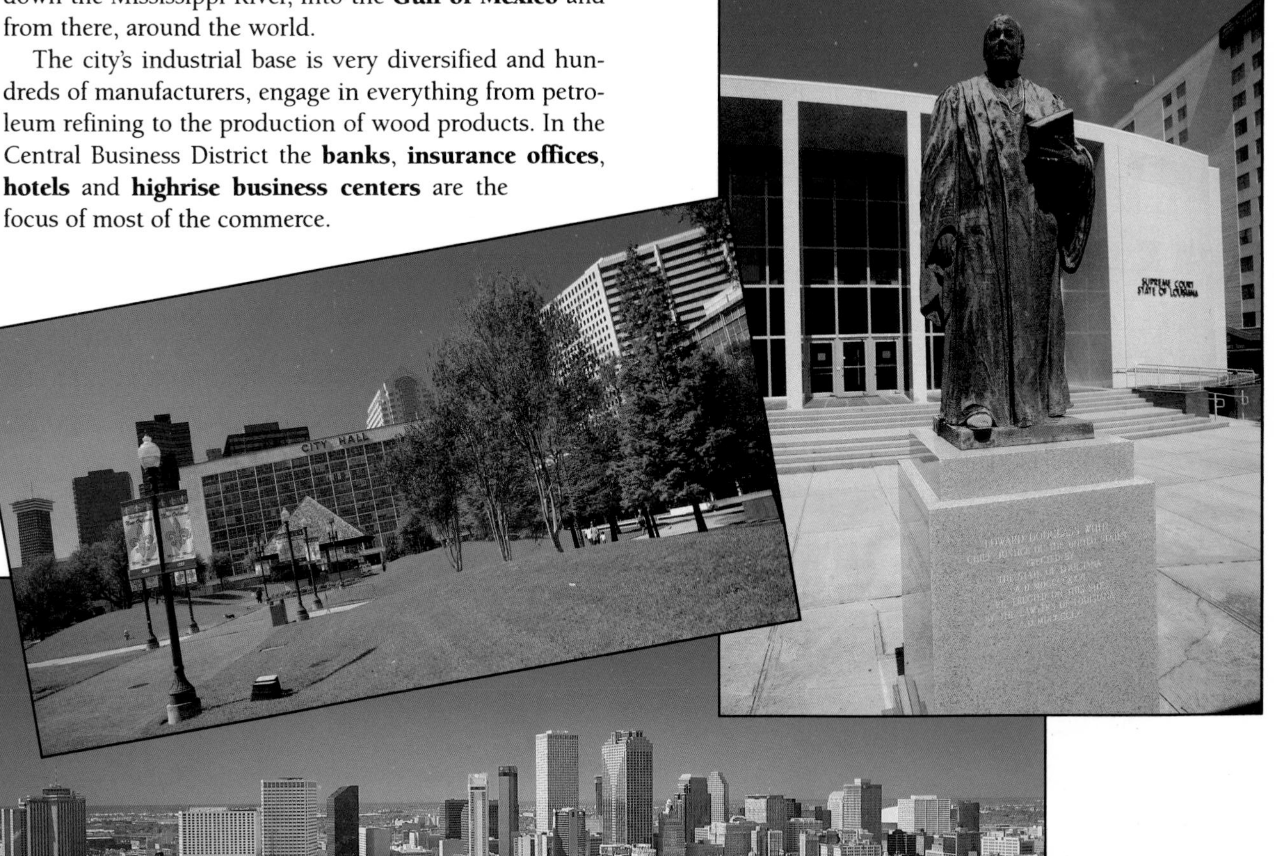

The Central Business District, with its high rise office blocks, is the commercial heart of New Orleans.

The Spanish Plaza is landscaped with mosaic tiles, statues and a fountain which shoots water 50 feet into the air.

The statue of Joan of Arc, representing France, stands in the Spanish Plaza in front of the World Trade Center.

At the bottom of Canal Street, facing the river, is the World Trade Center and the Spanish Plaza. A bronze statue of **Bernardo de Galves**, the Spanish governor of Louisiana in the 1780s, guards the entrance. Around the plaza are two other statues representing Great Britain and France. The former is commemorated by a statue of **Sir Winston Churchill**. The latter, by **Joan of Arc**, mounted on a horse.

MERCHANT MARINE OUTFITTERS
RED WING SHOES
SAFETY
FRIEDBERGS
MENS WEAR

GARDEN DISTRICT

The Garden District is upriver from the CBD and the French Quarter, and it certainly lives up to its name. Settled by wealthy Americans after the Louisiana Purchase, this neighborhood boasts huge, **antebellum mansions** surrounded by **manicured gardens**.

The elaborate homes are quite different from the small, elegant townhouses of the French Quarter and when they were built, the entrenched Creole society looked down their noses at such displays of vanity. The snobbish Creoles thought it quite unseemly that "new" American entrepreneurs and wheeler-dealers should show off their wealth in such an obvious fashion. Vulgar though they may have seemed to the cultured Creoles, these well-heeled citizens left an architectural legacy of magnificent estates.

The biggest stretch of greenery in the Garden District is the 385-acre **Audubon Park**, a public space where New Orleanians enjoy the great outdoors. Within its boundaries lies the **Audubon Zoological Garden**, considered one of the best zoos in North America.

There is a lot to see at the garden, including alligators, otters, turtles and exotic birds. More than 1,800 animals live in this natural habitat of rocks, trees and trenches. The zoo is a research center where endangered animals are bred, as well as a place to display flora and fauna.

The Audubon Zoological Garden features the Louisiana Swamp Exhibit which highlights the flora and fauna of the region.

Typical of the antebellum architectural style, are the balconies and doorways flanked by pillars which adorn the antebellum mansions of the Garden District.

UNIVERSITIES

ACROSS FROM AUDUBON PARK ARE THE CITY'S TWO oldest universities, **Loyola** and **Tulane**. Loyola was established by the **Jesuits** in 1837. It started as a small boarding school and when it became a university in 1912, attracted only a few dozen students. Today its enrollment is around 5,000. Loyola is particularly known for its communications department which is housed in a grand, Gothic-style building.

Tulane University was founded as a privately-run medical school in 1834 and today is comprised of 11 colleges and schools. Among the over 900 faculty are an impressive number of **Rhodes Scholars**. Many educators consider Tulane to be on a par with **Harvard** and **Princeton**.

Tulane, while still a medical school, is also known for its law school and magnificent library. The central building, **Gibson Hall**, dates back to the turn of the century. More modern buildings are scattered around the campus, including the **Sophie H. Newcomb College for Women**.

New Orleans has two other centers of higher learning, **Xavier University of Louisiana** and the **University of New Orleans**. Xavier was founded in 1915 as a school for black and native Americans. Xavier offers degrees in pharmacy, theology and education.

The University of New Orleans, with over 20,000 students from 46 states and 75 countries, is Louisiana's second largest educational institution. The graduate school offers 13 doctoral programs and 43 masters programs in the arts, science, music, public administration, education and urban and regional planning.

Tulane University is a private educational institution. It was named after Paul Tulane, a New Orleans merchant.

The campus of the University of New Orleans is the most modern of the universities in the area. It was founded in 1958.

Xavier University of Louisiana is known for its College of Pharmacy, and is one of four institutions of higher learning in New Orleans.

Loyola University takes its name from Saint Ignatius of Loyola who founded The Order of Jesus, more commonly called the Jesuits.

Sheraton
Marriott
CAJUN
QUEEN

Cemeteries in New Orleans have been dubbed "the cities of the dead," because the above-ground vaults and mausoleums almost look like buildings.

CEMETERIES

THERE AREN'T TOO MANY PLACES WHERE CEMETERIES ARE tourist attractions, but in New Orleans they are a major draw. Visitors can even take walking tours around the burial grounds and learn something about the colorful characters who rest there.

The 85-foot **Moriarty monument** in the **Metairie Cemetery**, for example, is the final resting place of a lady who was the wife of a poor Irish immigrant. Although her husband became a successful businessman, he was never accepted into New Orleans' snobbish high society. When his wife died in 1887, **Mr. Moriarty** was determined that she should "look down her nose" at the people who had snubbed her.

The older graves in New Orleans are all above-ground. Because the city has a high water table and sits below sea level, people could not be buried underground — their coffins would quickly float to the surface. The technical difficulties have been eliminated with modern burial methods, but many families still prefer the elaborate **above-ground tombs** and vaults which dot the city's cemetaries.

As with their homes, the aristocratic Creoles tried to outdo one another when burying their dead. Some of the family vaults are as fancy as the houses built for the living.

The Spanish and French upper classes spared no expense when building a burial place for their loved ones. Many of the tombs are built of marble, embellished with urns, crosses and statues.

LAKEVIEW

City Park is in Lakeview, the district which borders **Lake Pontchartrain**. The 1500-acre park used to be a sugar plantation owned by the **Allard family**, and is now one of the biggest tracts of municipal greenery in the United States. It encompasses the New Orleans Museum of Art, tennis courts, a golf course, a children's entertainment area, sports stadiums and numerous hiking trails and picnic areas.

Also within the grounds of **City Park** is the **New Orleans Botanical Garden**. Landscaped with fountains and sculptures designed by **Enrique Alferez**, the botanical garden has a tropical conservatory, a formally laid-out rose garden and beds of azaleas and camelias. Gardening fans can find books on horticultural subjects at the educational center and gift shop.

Those who love flowers and plants will also enjoy **Longvue House and Gardens**. Situated south of City Park, this beautiful estate was the home of **Edith** and **Edgar Stern**. She was a Sears heiress and her husband was a weathy cotton broker. No expense was spared in creating what looks like a transplanted English country home. The **Greek Revival mansion** is filled with priceless antiques and the gardens are landscaped with different themes. One section is fashioned after the **Generalife Gardens** of the **Alhambra** in Spain.

Lake Pontchartrain, a shallow, brackish inland estuary of the Mississippi River, sprawls over 625 square miles. The lake is ringed by resorts, miles of seawall and two state parks. New Orleanians head to the lake on hot humid days because the air is cooler than in the downtown area. The south shore of the lake is linked to the north by the 24-mile-long **Lake Pontchartrain Causeway**, the longest bridge over water in the world.

The Louisiana Native Garden at Longvue House is one of several themed areas. The garden show cases camellias and other local plants.

City Park is twice the size of New York's Central Park and is one of the oldest green urban spaces in the United States.

Houmas House Plantation and Gardens was built in stages, between the early 19th century and 1840. A massive estate, it went through economic ups and downs. The plantation boomed after John Burnside, an Irish planter, bought it in 1857.

PLANTATIONS

A COUPLE OF CENTURIES AGO, PLANTATIONS WERE VERY much part of the Louisiana landscape. More than just tropical farms, they were **huge estates** with rambling mansions and acres of greenery where crops like **cotton**, **tobacco**, **rice** and **sugar** were cultivated by hundreds of slaves. The plantation era reached its zenith in the 17th and 18th centuries when cheap black labor was readily available. After the **American Civil War** and the **emancipation of slaves** in 1863, the plantation system started to crumble, but many of the homes remained and the land was still worked by impoverished sharecroppers.

Oak Alley is from the old plantations era, and like most of the plantation homes, is located outside the city. The stately old trees which it was named after were planted as early as the 1700s. The house was constructed later, in 1836. Oak Alley is one of the most handsome plantation mansions in the American South and it attracts over 70,000 visitors per year.

The plantation homes that are open to the public are scattered around the **Great River Road**, which winds from **New Orleans** to **Baton Rouge**, along the shores of the Mississippi River. The route is an easy daytrip from New Orleans, but not if you want to cover more than one or two properties. The plantations are much too big to be explored in a couple of hours, visitors take at least half a day to tour each one.

Nottoway is the largest of all, with an astounding 64 rooms and 200 windows. Recently refurbished (it was built in 1859), the **Greek Revival Italianate** mansion is aptly nicknamed "**The White Castle**" and gives visitors a taste of how wealthy plantation owners lived. The ballroom is a formal, elegant chamber hung with crystal

San Francisco House features five ornately hand-painted ceilings and faux marbling on the fireplaces and woodwork.

Many plantation homes, including San Francisco, had large marble fireplaces, which seems extraordinary given Louisiana's hot and humid climate.

chandeliers — it isn't hard to imagine gracious ladies clad in long gowns, tripping around the dance floor with their debonair beaux.

Nottoway was considered very modern for its time. The house, which sprawls over 53,000 square feet, had hot and cold running water, gas lighting and coal-burning fireplaces with marble mantlepieces. The rich interior is lavishly decorated with plaster friezes, antiques and hand-painted, porcelain door handles.

The **San Francisco Plantation** in **Reserve**, on the north bank of the Mississippi, is not as elegant as Nottoway but no expense has been spared on its decoration. Constructed in 1856 by **Edmond Bozonier Marmillion**, it was built in an ornate style known as **Steamboat Gothic**. The family spent a fortune on the ceiling frescoes and the fussy, gingerbread trim.

Destrehan Plantation is quite close to town. It's at the southern end of the Great River Road, near the **New Orleans International Airport**. Completed in 1787, it is the oldest of all the plantation homes and is built in a simple style similar to those found in the **West Indies**. The pirate **Jean Lafitte** was said to have stayed here on several occasions.

Destrehan Plantation House was built when the Spanish still ruled over New Orleans. Louisiana had not yet become part of the United States. In 1788, when the mansion was still under construction, George Washington was elected as the first president of the fledgling nation.

The sweet scent of magnolia and guides dressed like southern belles welcome visitors to **Houmas House Plantation and Gardens**, a restored, antebellum home built in 1840. Houmas House, which lies between Oak Alley and Nottoway, is a Greek Revival mansion famous for its three-story spiral staircase. The plantation home has been used as a backdrop in several **movies** about the American South.

Although by today's standards Houmas House seems impossibly grand, it used to be even larger. It was built by **Colonel John Smith Preston** of **South Carolina** who oversaw a 10,000-acre estate run by hundreds of workers. Unmarried men lived in "bachelors' quarters," alongside the mansion.

Tezcuco (the name comes from an Aztec word meaning "quiet place") is another Greek Revival home. It's not far from Houmas House and was built 15 years later, but it is much smaller — a "raised cottage" in local parlance. It isn't exactly a shack, however. Tezcuco's rooms average more than 600 square-feet. The plasterwork around its lofty ceilings are richly ornamental, reflecting the fashion in the mid-19th century.

Nottoway is near the community of White Castle. The plantation home, which is ringed by 22 Doric columns, has earned the same nickname.

Nottoway's rose garden has been turned into a swimming pool and the mansion has been extensively restored. The interior is richly furnished with velvet drapes, gilt-framed mirrors and chandeliers.

A sun-dappled lane lined with moss-draped trees leads to the aptly-named Oak Alley Plantation. The quarter-mile long walkway has been the backdrop for many movies about the historic American South. Strolling towards the handsome house with its 28 classical columns, it's easy to feel transported into the past. ▶

Tezcuco Plantation Home is not as grand as some of its neighbors along the River Road, but it is certainly one of the fanciest bed and breakfasts in Louisiana. Guests can stay in a luxurious suite or in cottages on the grounds.

BAYOUS & CAJUN COUNTRY

FEW THINGS CONJUR UP THE LANDSCAPE OF LOUSIANA more readily than its swamps, marshlands and bayous (a native Indian word for "creek"). Teeming with birds, reptiles and insects, they are hot, humid and fragrant — mysterious backwaters where nature has the upper hand. Ancient cypress trees draped with moss rise from the water like the gnarled fingers of witches. Lurking between the palms, are alligators, egrets and an assortment of other creatures who make this watery kingdom their home.

"**Cajun Country**" is in the heart of this wilderness, to the west of New Orleans. The **Cajuns**, or **Acadians**, as they were originally known, were fishermen and farmers from New France, (primarily **Nova Scotia** and **New Brunswick**) who were thrown off their land by the **British** in 1755. Many moved south to Louisiana, chosing to live in the back country where they could live in peace, away from the hustle and bustle of New Orleans.

Like the Creole aristocracy, the Cajuns were **French** speaking, but they were poor, ill-educated, folk who didn't have much in common with the snobbish high society of New Orleans. They founded their own settlements in this back country, building simple homes by the edge of the rivers and bayous.

Today some Cajuns continue the tradition of their forebears, living off the land, by trapping and fishing, but their name has come to mean more than a way of life. The term "Cajun" is applied to a spicy, regional cuisine and to toe-tapping music featuring fiddles and stuttering accordions. Cajuns don't need much of an excuse to throw a party. In **Lafayette**, the Cajun "capital," and in the hamlets that dot the area, visitors can usually find a festival or two.

Vacationers can drive along the roads which wind around the bayous, but the best way to explore Cajun Country is by boat. Local fishermen use flat-bottomed crafts to glide into the swamps without getting tangled in the undergrowth. Visitors can take a sightseeing tour on an air boat which skims along the water, without harming the vegetation.

The bayous of Louisiana are a fisherman's paradise. Boats, fishing gear, licenses and guides can be rented in the 800,000-acre Atchafalaya Basin, 15 miles east of Lafayette in Cajun Country.

Flowers and trees flourish in the hot, humid climate.

Visitors are often surprised to spot an alligator, peacefully wallowing in the water only inches from their boat.

Palm trees and moss-shrouded cypresses line the banks of the bayous.

White egrets and bald eagles live and feed in the bayous of Louisiana.

Suzanne
E
Saunders
original
paintings
DOWN

New Orleans has the kind of personality which imposes itself upon visitors in subtle and delightful ways. Tourists encounter its history and colorful culture in the architecture, the spicy Creole and Cajun cooking, the friendly, easy-going manner of its citizens and, of course, in the music.

Music is the heartbeat of New Orleans. Even during the rare times when there isn't a festival going on, there's always something to celebrate — the past, the present, the future.